DR CALMAN'S

Dictionary of Psychoanalysis

By the same author

Bed-Sit (*Jonathan Cape*)
Boxes (*Jonathan Cape*)
Calman & Women (*Jonathan Cape*)
My God (*Souvenir Press*)
The Penguin Calman
The New Penguin Calman
This Pestered Isle (*Times Books*)
Couples (*The Workshop*)

Printed and bound in Great Britain by Butler & Tanner Ltd, Frome and London, for the publishers, W. H. Allen & Co. Ltd. 44 Hill Street, London W1X 8LB

ISBN 0 491 02296 4

DR CALMAN'S
Dictionary of Psychoanalysis

MEL CALMAN

W.H.ALLEN - LONDON
A Howard & Wyndham Company
1979

DEDICATION

To Professor Kreplach – with ambivalence

Aggression

I'm delighted
to see you're
now able to
express your
aggressions....

Ambivalence

Amnesia

Analyst

Anger

Animus & Anima

Anxiety

Which is it to be today?
Phobic, castration,
separation,
depressive,
paranoid anxiety
or plain
panic?

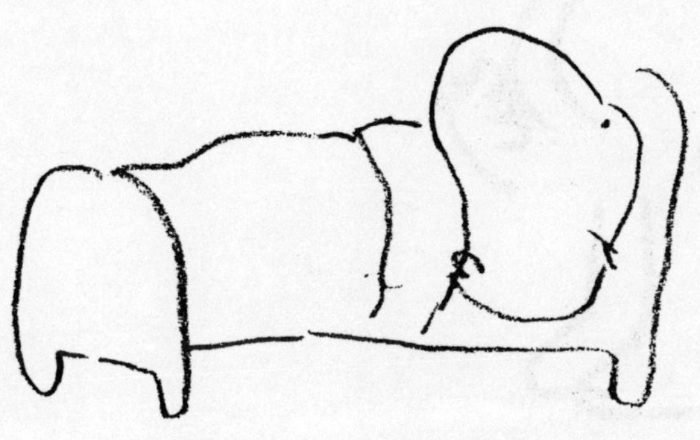

Bisexual

Breast

I love a good breast...
Does he mean that in the Kleinian sense or the carnal?

Castration Anxiety

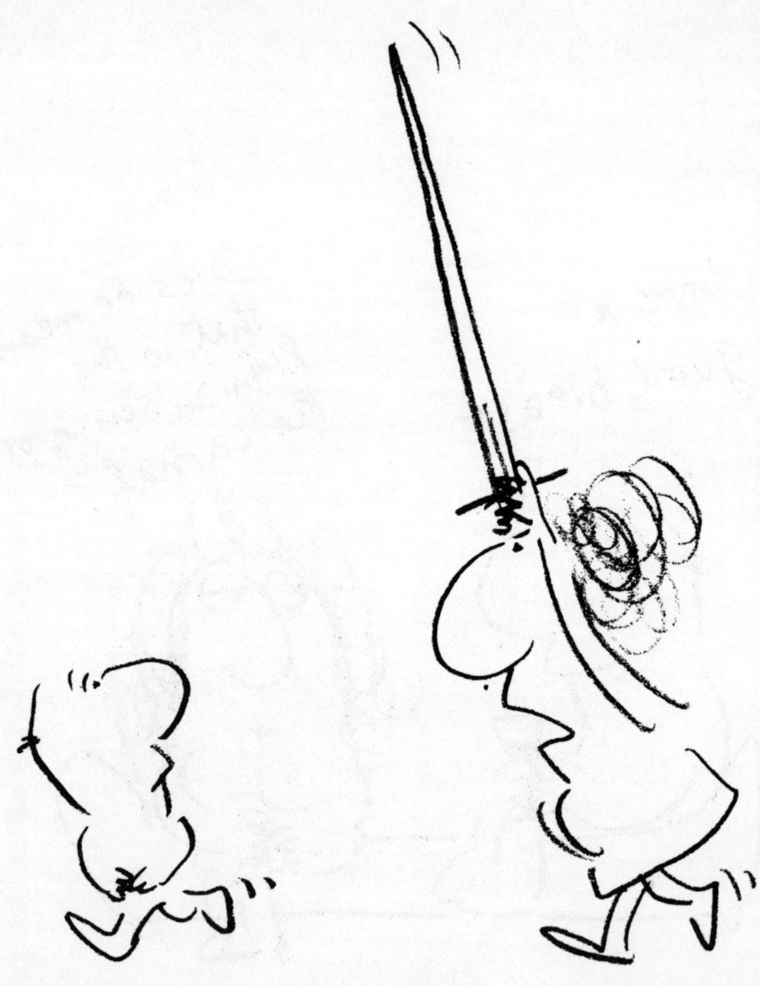

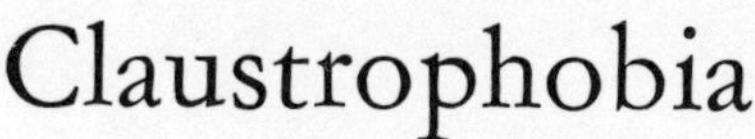

Claustrophobia

Coitus

Communication

One of my problems is that
I have trouble in communicating..
It seems I find myself using words
as a defence.. they are a shield
behind which I hide.. I don't believe
in the reality of feelings.. so I try
to verbalize my inner conflicts
and this results in a schizoid
dichotomy between my guts and
my head.. Do you follow me?
Do you find I cannot
communicate properly?
Well?

Compulsive

Conflict

This is either a bad case of conflict or a man with two wives: Editor.

Death Wish

Depression

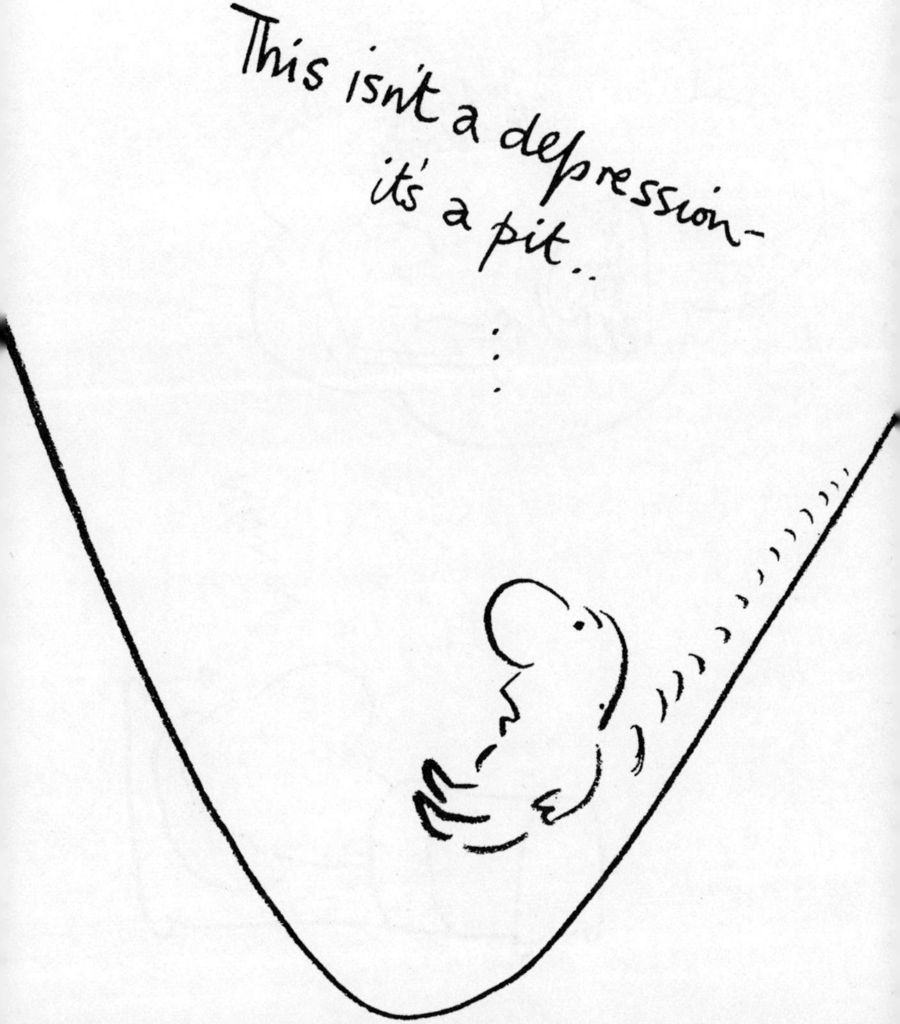

This isn't a depression–
it's a pit...

Dreams

Ego

Exhibitionism

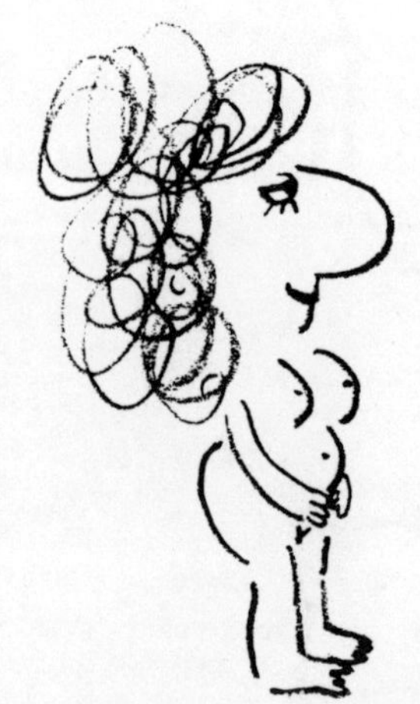

Fantasy

Father

I'm not your father-figure –
I'm your father!

Fear

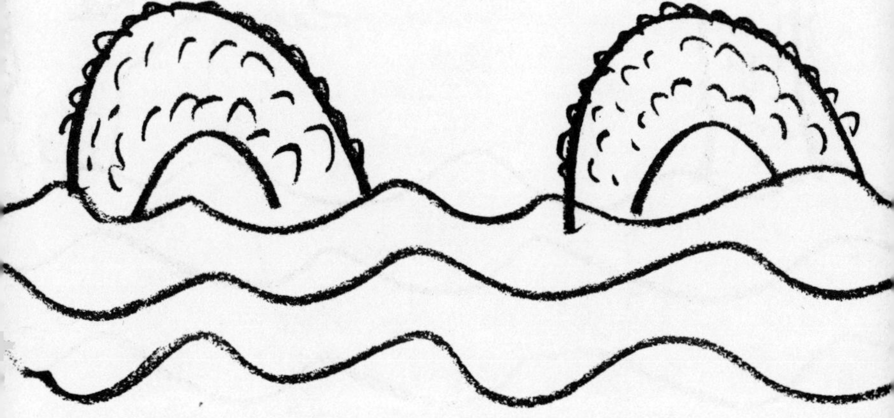

Fetish

Fixation

Forgetting

I don't care if it was unconscious - you shouldn't have forgotten my birthday ..

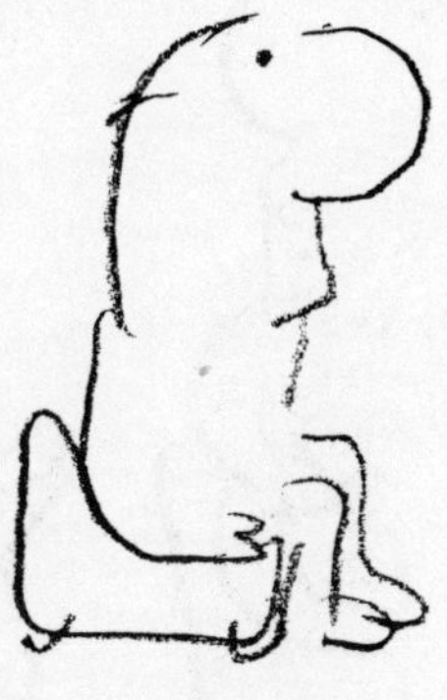

Free Association

Freedom

Freudian Slip

Frigidity *(see Headaches)*

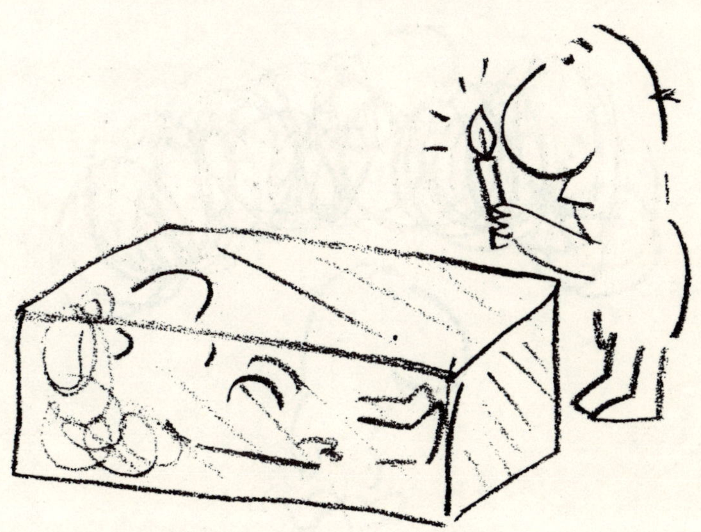

Gloom *(see Melancholia)*

Guilt

And now
I feel guilty
that I feel
so guilty
about everything

Happiness

What are the symptoms of happiness, Doctor?

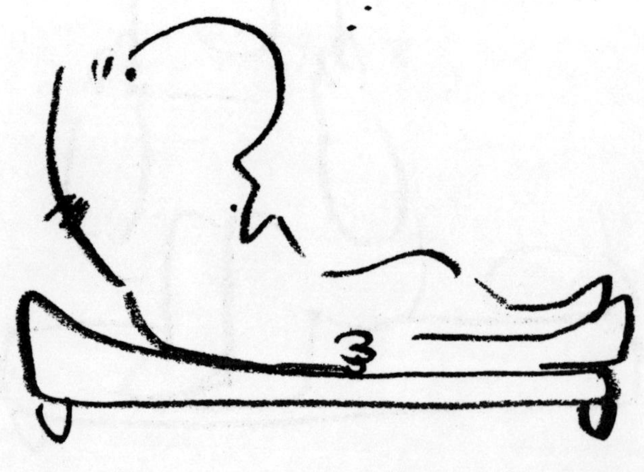

Hate

Never mind
the ambivalence -
what about
the HATE ?

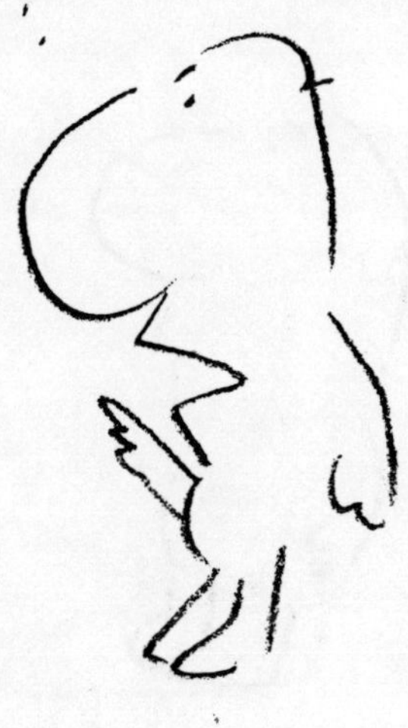

Hostility

I'm not really into
hostility right now –
but I'll kick you
if you like

Hypochondria

Even hypochondriacs get ill . .

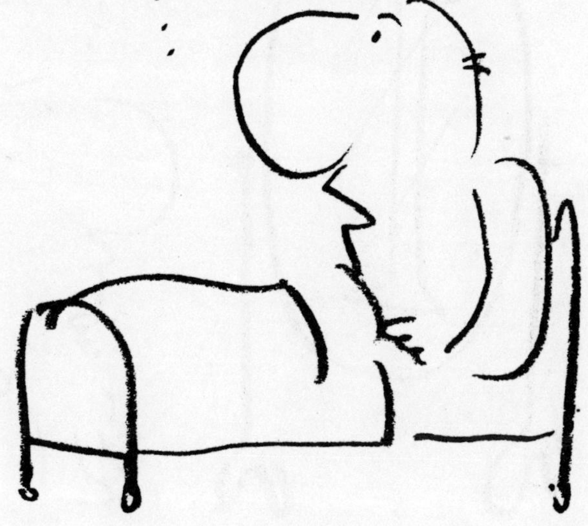

I

Id

Identity

Who am I?
I am ME. But is ME
really 'me' or just someone
who goes to an analyst
and has a wife and children
and his own overdraft?
And if I'm not me – who will
I be when I grow up... on the other
hand if I can keep away
from the cracks in the
pavements, I'll be
O.K... Please God.
If I believe in GOD..
whoever He is.. Oh GOD-
I'm late for my next
appointment..

Identity Crisis

Incest

She's not just old enough to be his mother –
she is...

Infantile Regression

Insanity

Jealousy

Libido

Love

When you say 'LOVE'
do you mean EROS or
a need for instinctual
satisfaction or object love
or oedipal love
or genital love
or simple old-fashioned
schmaltz?

Marriage *(see Help!)*

Doctor-
I'm suffering from
bouts of marriage..

Masochism

I had to give up
masochism –
I was enjoying it
too much . . .

Masturbation

Mature

Melancholia *(see Depression)*

Mind

it's something
I'm always out of...

Mother *(see Oedipus Complex)*

Narcissism

Negative

I'm not being negative – I'm saying 'No' ...

Neurotic

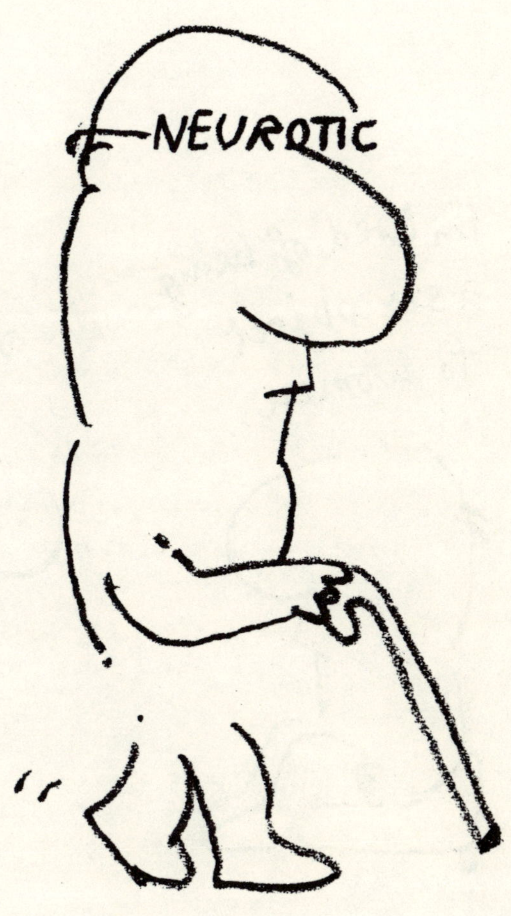

Object

I'm tired of being a sex object to women..

Obsession

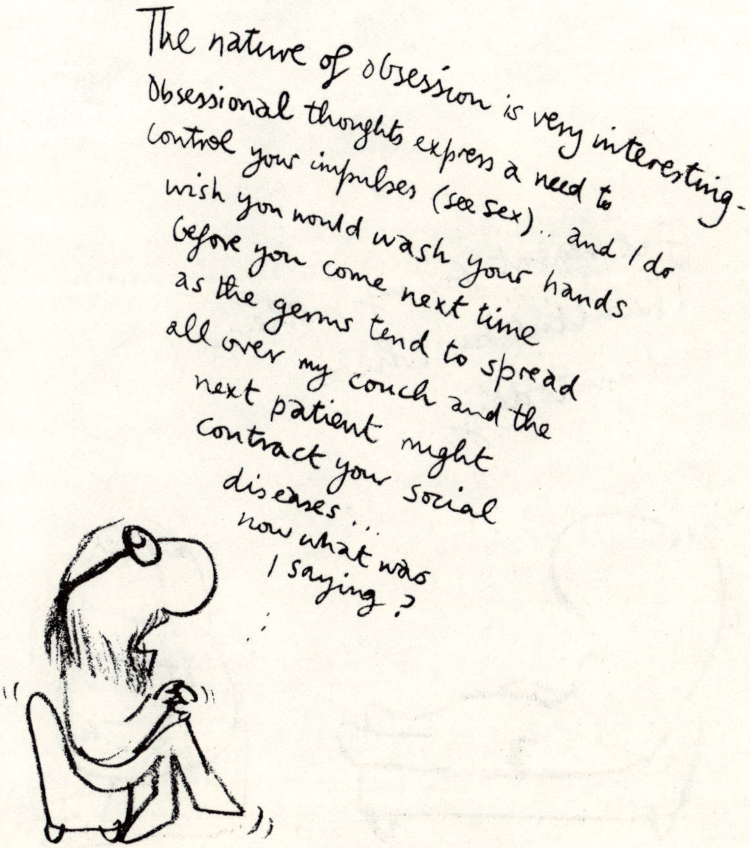

The nature of obsession is very interesting-
Obsessional thoughts express a need to
control your impulses (see sex).. and I do
wish you would wash your hands
before you come next time
as the germs tend to spread
all over my couch and the
next patient might
contract your social
diseases...
now what was
I saying?

Oedipus Complex *(see Mother)*

If it wasn't for my mother –
I wouldn't be where
I am today . .

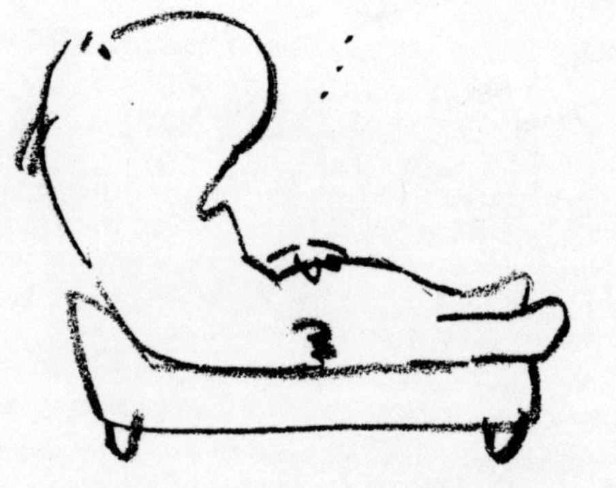

Orgasm

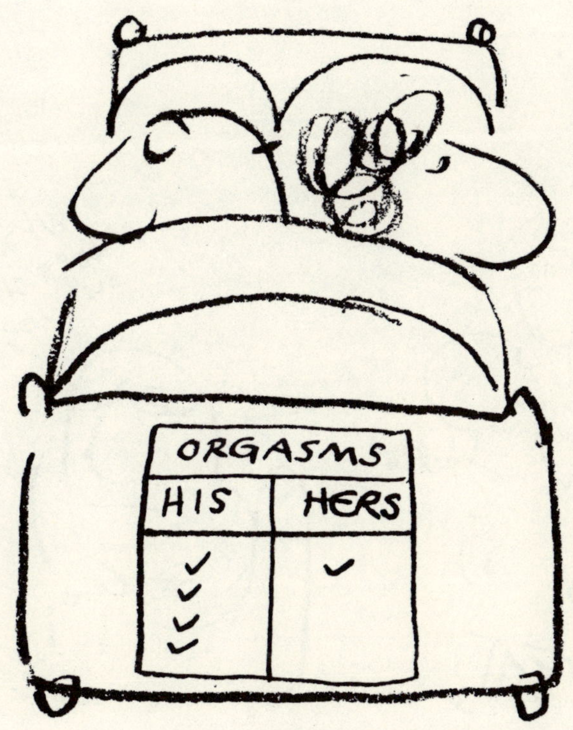

Paranoia

Patient

I hope I'm not boring you

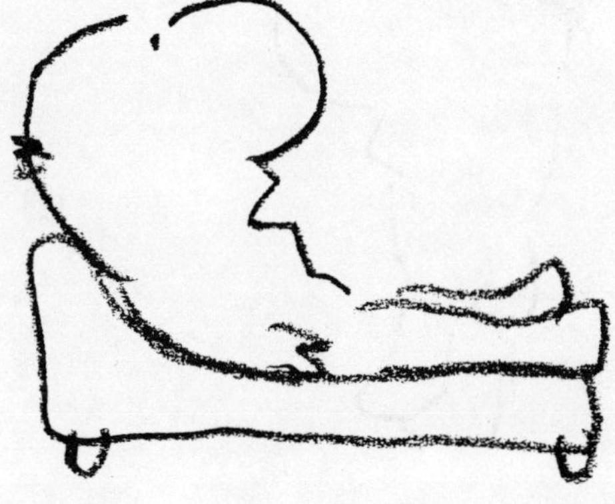

Penis Envy

Well-can't I borrow it just for tonight?

Persona

Phallic Symbol

I dreamed of
a tall, dark man
last night

It's probably
phallic...

Phobia

Pleasure

Pleasure Principle

Projection

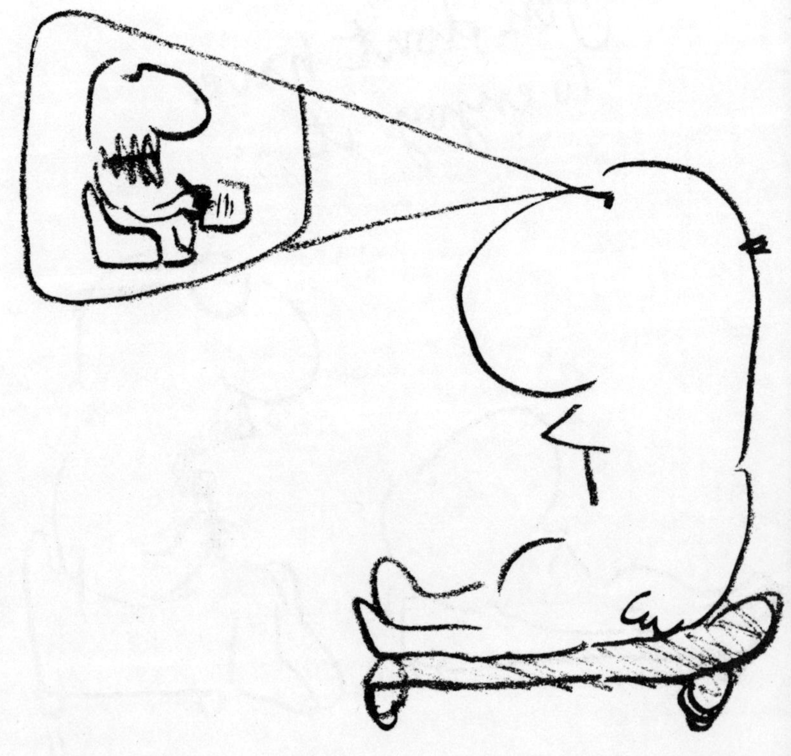

Psyche

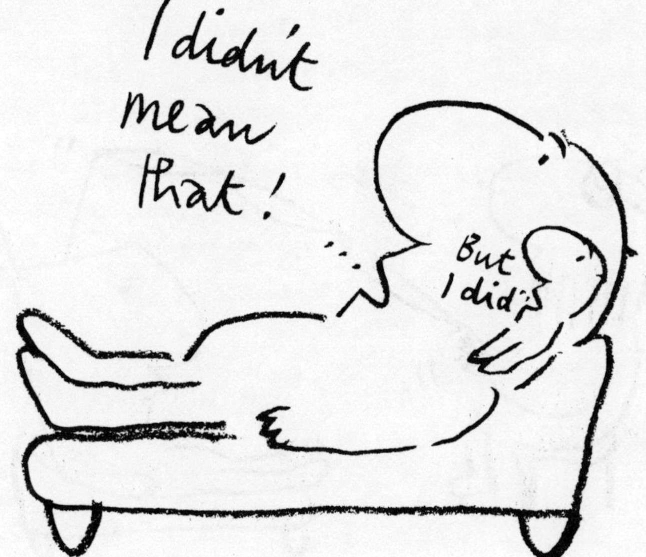

Psychoanalysis

Psychosis

Psychosomatic

Rapport

Real

Is this real –
and if so – why does it
cost so much?

Reality

If it hurts –
it's real . . .

Religion

Repression

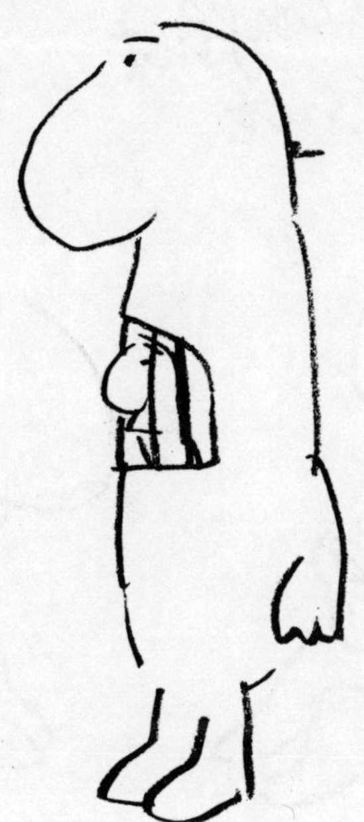

Sadness *(see Gloom, Depression)*

Separation Anxiety

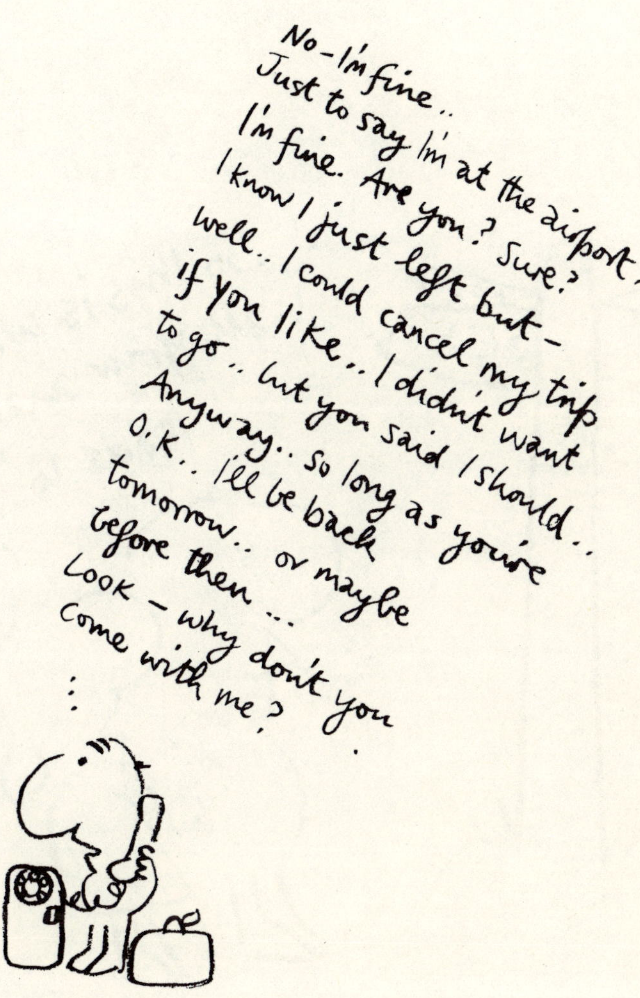

Sex

Sexual Perversion

I dont mind dressing up as a chicken – but I'm damned if I'm going to lay eggs for her

Superego

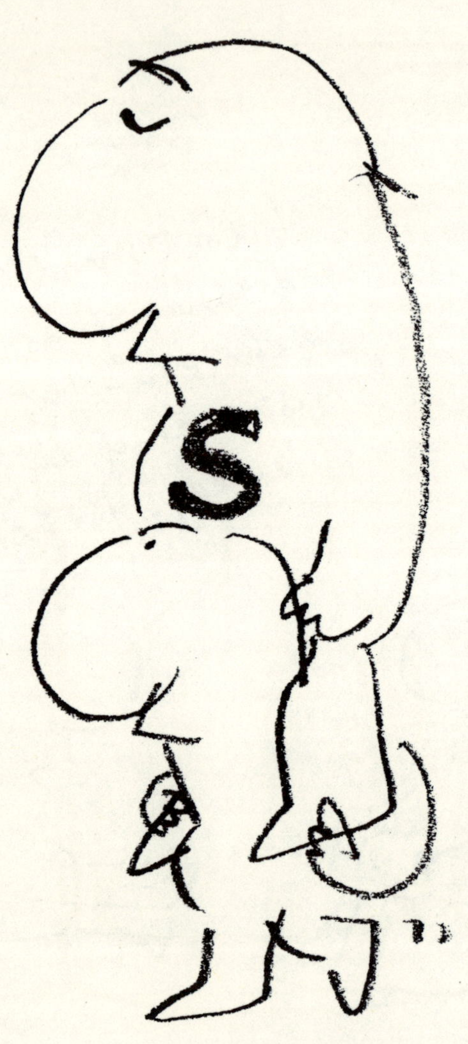

Time

Transference

You now even look like my mother!

Transvestite

I don't mind you wearing my dress - but I do mind you getting more wolf whistles in it..

Trauma

I come from
a long line of
traumas..

Truth

I'm coming out —
whether I like it
or not

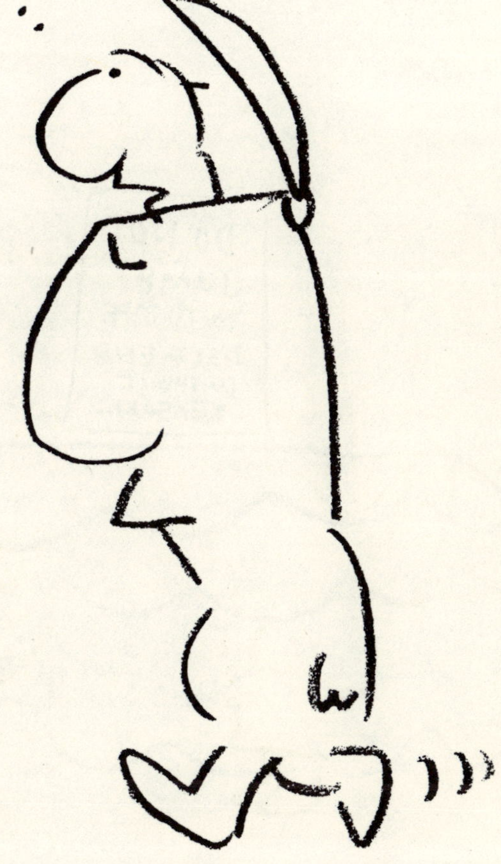

Unconscious, The

DEEP
END